Now What?

THE **7 VITAL STEPS** TO SELF-PUBLISH
YOUR MANUSCRIPT

ABIGAIL TURNER

PipStones

"Weavers of Tales and Tellers of Truth"

PipStones Publishing
P.O. Box 4507
Fort Walton Beach, Florida 32549
www.pipstones.com

Now What? The 7 Vital Steps to Self-Publish your Manuscript
Copyright ©2024 PipStones, LLC.

Author: Abigail Turner
Editors: Abigail Turner & Deborah Hoffman

Library of Congress Control Number: 2024948798
Copyright ©2024
Published in 2024

ISBN-13: 979-8-9889427-3-3, Print
ISBN-13: 979-8-9889427-4-0, Ebook

For Worldwide Distribution.
Printed in The United States of America.

Welcome Page

Welcome to your easy-to-follow handbook to help make your book a success! Thank you for traveling this journey with us and seeing your importance in the self-publishing world. Your stories can make a difference, and our goal is for your book to be planted into the hands of many readers!

My name is Abby. I am the co-owner of PipStones Publishing, and like you, I am also an author. PipStones provides author services in editing, book design, publishing, distribution, local marketing, social marketing, and training.

Go to www.pipstones.com/contact to view more information about our company, or to set up a complimentary consultation. You can also read our About section at the end of this book with information to download FREE Bonus PDFs.

In these 7 impactful steps, I will walk you through the essentials of moving your words on paper to a fully published book. From manuscript to the store, this guide has it all! Pay close attention to the questions, information, and HINT sections at the end of each step. This information will save you from many headaches and prevent expensive errors!

Thank you for allowing us to help you in your literary journey!

All information in this book is for educational purposes only. In no manner is PipStones, LLC endorsing any particular companies or businesses.

Abigail Turner

PipStones Publishing

Contents

1. Step 1: Seeds   1

2. Step 2: Stones   4

3. Step 3: Stems   11

4. Step 4: Blooms   16

5. Step 5: Planters   20

6. Step 6: Sun   24

7. Step 7: Growth   30

8. Now What? Process   32

Author Biography   41

Also by Abigail Turner   43

About PipStones Publishing   47

Step 1: Seeds

❦

Congratulations! You've accomplished a task that many other writers don't—completing the body of your manuscript! You may ask, "What do I do now?" Well, you're not alone with that question. When we began this journey of self-publishing, we were in your shoes. We didn't have the keys or knowledge to edit our manuscripts properly, we didn't know how to publish, where to go for distribution, and we had no idea how to market our books. It took hours, months, and years to research the information and do it correctly in a growing market! That is why we have made it our goal to help you!

Our mission at PipStones Publishing is to market and publish unique and refreshing works from various authors and genres, presenting and highlighting their literary endeavors in an ever-changing marketplace.

The foundational seeds of your manuscript are essential to the success of your book. Here is a breakdown of the necessary parts and pieces to begin your self-publishing journey. If you've already done this, then you're further than most. Great job! If that's the case, you can move to Step 2.

The Full Manuscript

1. Your manuscript's body needs to be intact. At this point, I'm sure you have reviewed and reread the body many times to ensure that it is free of obvious errors.

2. Ensure your manuscript is typed into a Word or Google Document and saved on a desktop or laptop. Compiling your manuscript using your phone is inefficient. I suggest downloading Microsoft Office or getting familiar with Google Docs if you haven't already done that.

3. Go to www.microsoft.com to obtain a free trial and click on Microsoft 365.

4. Complete the necessary material for your book.

Title Page
Copyright Page
Dedication
Acknowledgments
Table of Contents
Introduction (my introduction is labeled Welcome Page)
Forward
Prologue
Preface
Body (all main chapters)
Afterward
Appendices, Glossary, Bibliography, Resources, Index
Biography (with author photo)
Back Cover Blurb (what entices the reader to buy the book)
Editorial Review/s (for the back cover)
Back Cover Author Biography (only a snippet)

5. If you are not computer literate, find someone who is. Everything for your book is digitally accepted. The era of handwritten or paper manuscript submissions is now obsolete.

6. Type each piece into a separate document file and be specific when naming the file (i.e., Backcoverblurb1, Biography1, Resources1).

7. Save everything for the interior of your book into one folder (i.e., Interior Drafts).

8. To pull each file quickly, create individual files within the Interior Drafts folder (i.e., Biography, Back Cover Blurb, Table of Contents). This will make your editing process much more efficient and eliminate confusion.

9. For editing, keep each file separate, but compile your final drafts into one document before designing the book.

Question:
What parts will you include in your book?

HINT: Some Table of Contents items may be optional for your book. Choose only the necessary parts, and don't sweat over the rest.

Step 2: Stones

～～

This step is the process of editing. You may think of editing as a rocky road, but it is necessary for the success of your book. I will share the DOs and DON'Ts to hiring an editor and give you resources to begin editing your manuscript. You will have a beautifully polished piece when you finish, and your manuscript's rough parts will be smooth and shiny.

WARNING!
Please, please, please, do not take a friend's word over an actual editor that your book is done being edited or that it appears free from errors!

Just as you apply your expertise in another job to enhance the efficiency of the company, an editor brings the same level of professionalism to your book. An editor not only refines your manuscript to improve its quality but also plays a crucial role in boosting your sales and minimizing the risk of negative reviews. By ensuring that your book is polished and error-free, an editor helps streamline your path to success as an author. If you can afford it, investing in an editor is highly recommended. Consider saving for this essential service and prioritizing it in your budget—a valuable investment in your writing career.

I can't express how frequently I encounter authors who have had their books edited by another company, only to feel that the final product no longer captures their original vision. This can happen, but it doesn't have to. Drawing from my experience editing numerous successful books, I'm here to provide the essential steps that will help make your editing choices clearer and equip you with the knowledge to enhance and refine your manuscript.

DOs & DON'Ts To Hiring An Editor:

DO Ask Questions!

1. What is your pricing? Editing can be costly, so be prepared to tell them what your budget may be.

2. How long is the process?

3. What type of editing will I receive for that price point?

4. Can you send me a short sample of a "before and after" from a book that you edited?

5. How many rounds of editing will we be doing together?

6. Will you edit all the extra material for my manuscript? Is that included in the price?

7. What are your methods of payment, and how frequently do I pay?

8. When can I receive a contract to sign?

9. What is the general timeline for this process?

10. If I hire you, when can we begin?

DON'T Hire The Editor...

1. If *you* haven't worked on editing your book first. When I give estimates for editing, I weigh them depending on how much work I feel the book will need. The less editing, the better the price.

2. If they tell you how many rounds of editing you will receive. Their answer should be, "Until it is complete, and you are satisfied."

3. If they tell you to pay in total upfront. There should be a split payment: one to begin and one upon finishing. A middle payment can even be included.

4. If you cannot speak to them on the phone. You should have regular meetings or the option to set up a call when necessary.

5. If they didn't respond to your original call for services promptly. I wouldn't even consider hiring them.

6. If they are unclear on the process or type of editing or won't provide a reasonable timeline.

7. If they don't provide you with a contract.

8. If their prices seem unreasonable. But, yes, editing can be expensive. Don't think you're not getting a bang for your buck because it's out of your price range. They also should provide you with an editing quote. You can sometimes negotiate the price, but I wouldn't "lowball" them. If they are a good editor, they probably have other clients that will pay them full price. So, conversing with them and telling them about your budget would be wise. Feel out the response they give you and weigh the waters.

9. If they aren't willing to send you a short sample of their editing beforehand.

10. If they won't send you a quote. Don't be impulsive on the phone. Wait to hear from them again with a quote. The timeliness of their proposal says a lot, too. Does it seem like they have time for you? Then, decide after that point.

11. If they <u>only</u> use programs or AI (Artificial Intelligence) for editing. There is nothing like a human to allow tone, feeling, and your voice to be heard throughout your book. After all, you want it to sound like *you* and not a computer, right? In self-publishing, AI is considered a "no, no." It can be used as a tool, but don't allow that to be your only means of editing.

Editing Prices

Pricing for editing services may vary. Some editors charge per word, page, or based on the number of chapters in the book. Others determine the price according to the specific type of editing required. Some editors may assess the price based on their perception of the book's needs or the author's requested process. It's important to carefully consider and compare these different pricing structures.

Editing Services

1. Manuscript Evaluation: A manuscript evaluation can be a great tool if you are an amateur author or a new writer in a specific genre. This is optional but recommended.

2. Copy Editing: This is the most basic type of editing, including spelling, grammar, and punctuation. Word choice can also be determined.

3. Line Editing: The second step in the editing process is to evaluate each line. This often requires rearranging and redesigning sentences and paragraphs.

4. Developmental Editing: This is a more in-depth type of editing. It requires more time and effort from you and the editor.

5. Professional Editing: This is a complete edit for your book.

6. Proofread: Proofreading is the final edit before your book's design and formatting. A separate person other than your general editor should proofread your manuscript. This person can be within the same company, but an individual eye on it is essential. After all, we are human and make mistakes, no matter how often we have looked at a manuscript.

You Can Edit Your Manuscript!

With all that information, you also have the option to edit your manuscript yourself. I strongly recommend this before handing it to a professional. Even with the resources below, you must be picky about accepting all edits from these programs. You still want it to sound like your voice, which is primary. For a more in-depth look at editing, see the About PipStones Publishing section toward the end of this book.

Use The Tools

1. In Word, you can click on the editor, which will guide you through the basics of copy editing and even some line editing. You should complete this process for each part of your book first.

2. Go to www.grammarly.com. You can use Grammarly for free to improve the files you edit.

3. If you want to go further, purchase the monthly or yearly Grammarly program. A more extended version allows you to dive deeper into the editing process. I highly suggest this.

4. Other valuable editing programs are Prowriting Aid, Autocrit, Scrivener, and Hemingway App. These all have different price points and options.

5. Get a thesaurus!!! This is a <u>must</u>, or at least use your search engine to look up alternate words and phrases.

6. A valuable book that I use is *The Chicago Manual of Style, Seventeenth Edition*.

7. Use these tools for ALL parts of your book.

8. Don't give up; this can be tedious. You've come so far already!

When you are ready to hire a professional editor, be aware that you will still be doing edits with them if they care about your book. Only a "good editor" will work with you. A "bad editor" will do all the edits and then hand it back without your input. And before you know it, the book doesn't sound like you! Please don't make that mistake, and above all, follow the items I have given you in this step when hiring an editor.

Information:
Create a list of editors you researched for your manuscript/genre.

_____

_____

_____

_____

_____

_____

_____

_____

_____

_____

HINT: Conduct as many necessary edits as needed for your book to complete it. However, at some point, you have to say, "Consummatum est"—"It is finished."

Step 3: Stems

After the foundational seeds have been planted and the stones polished, it's time to create the solid, beautiful stems. This step includes the design of your book. I will provide information to create your own cover and interior design, but you can also hire a professional.

This process is going to help your book stand out above the rest. I can't tell you how often an author has come to me and said, "I don't know why my book isn't making sales." Then, they show me their book cover or interior. Sometimes, I bite my tongue, and other times, I suggest they hire a designer or our company for those services. **In this business, we do judge a book by its cover, and so should you!** Don't settle for a less-than-awesome cover or dull interior design.

Interior Design

1. The same concepts apply to hiring a formatting designer as to hiring an editor. Be selective. I recommend hiring a formatter for your book if you have the funds.

2. Doing your own formatting requires much planning:

- Format in Microsoft Word, Google Docs, Vellum, Atticus, Adobe Illustrator, or Adobe InDesign.
- Choose only a couple of easily readable fonts that characterize the book (i.e., a swirly font might appeal to a young girl's chapter book, but a dripping or pointed font may work well for a murder mystery).
- Have consistent uniformity throughout. Each chapter should look the same; the dedication page and introduction page headings should be the same font; paragraphing uniformity should be the same (centered, left, right, justified). *Example: I had a variance in whether I used bullet points for the subsections or a lowercase outline letter with a parenthesis like this: a). As you can see, I chose bullet points so every subsection will have this uniformity.*
- Be thorough and even double-check the editing as you move through the book.
- Add cohesive images that make the book stand out. If possible, I suggest hiring an illustrator. You can also create your own images in Canva or purchase pictures from companies such as iPhotos or Shutterstock.

3. Once you have completed the formatting, print a copy for review. Then, go back and make the necessary changes.

Cover Design

Again, if this is in your budget (and it should be), you can hire a cover designer. This is your most important "Stem!"

Items To Prepare

1. Trim Sizes- specific genres have "standard" or "suggested" trim sizes (the dimensions of your print book). Choose wisely! Make sure the platforms you choose for distribution will print in those sizes.

2. Download the cover template from the printing company's website.

3. Use the template to begin your design.

Do-It-Yourself Cover Design

1. Canva

2. Adobe Illustrator

3. Adobe InDesign

4. Kindle Direct Publishing- used for publishing on Amazon

5. IngramSpark Book Building Tool- used for publishing on IngramSpark

Cover Design Companies

1. PipStones.com

2. Fiverr.com

3. Reedsy.com

4. Getcovers.com

5. Companies or freelancers on Facebook Writing Groups

6. Search Engine- type in "Cover Design" and then your genre

7. What will you need for the cover?

- **Front Cover:** Artwork, Title, Author, Illustrator name (optional and primarily for a children's book)
- The words "Written By" are outdated. Be creative, or only include the author's name on the front.
- **Spine (the edge that shows on a shelf):** Artwork wrapped from the front, Title, Author, Logo (optional)
- **Back Cover:** Artwork wrapped from the front and spine, Title, Blurb (basically what entices the reader to buy the book, similar to a summary, but not precisely), Logo (optional), 1-3 sentence Author Bio (optional), Editorial Review (optional), ISBN, and Barcode (see Step 4)
- Prepare the pieces for the back cover in advance. These should be edited before someone works on the cover.

Question:
What parts are you going to design yourself? What parts will you seek out a professional for?

Information:
List your design and illustrator professionals here.

HINT: Tutorials on navigating each formatting and cover design service are available on YouTube and other platforms.

Step 4: Blooms

You've come so far, and now you know the book looks fantastic! You are ready to learn about some fundamental aspects of the publishing process that are vital for distribution. Welcome to the garden of book logistics!

ISBNs & Barcodes

Your book must have an ISBN. This is a 13-digit number that identifies your book's metadata. ISBN stands for International Standard Book Number. You can obtain ISBNs from Bowker (suggested) or from many of the distribution platforms for free.

1. Your own ISBN can be used on any platform, and you won't need several; only one per format (edition). Your IMPRINT is in your own

ISBN (either your business name or personal name will be imprinted within your book's metadata as the publisher/owner, not Amazon or Barnes and Noble, etc.).

2. With this, you will either generate a barcode yourself if you are using a private printer to create your stockpile of books, or you can enter the ISBN, and the POD distributor (explanation in Step 5) will generate a barcode on the back of your book for free.

Remember, even if the distributor generates the barcode from your ISBN, the number belongs to you unless you get the free ISBN from the distributor.

3. You will include this number on your copyright page.

4. Go to **bowker.com** to purchase ISBNs and Barcodes. It is more cost-effective to buy in bulk unless you plan to write only one or two books.

5. You will need a separate ISBN for each edition (format) of your book (i.e., 1 for a print version, 1 for an audiobook, 1 for an ebook, etc.).

LCCNs

The LCCN, or Library of Congress Control Number, is a 10-digit number used to catalog books within the Library of Congress of the United States. To receive an LCCN, you can open a PCN (Preassigned Control Number) account through the Library of Congress.

1. This is not required but allows libraries to search for your book quickly and include it in their system and on their shelves.

2. The PCN program allows you to receive this number in approximately 2 weeks. You must also be accepted as a PCN account holder, which takes approximately 2-4 weeks.

3. You will include your LCCN on your copyright page.

4. After publication, you will send a printed copy to the LOC (Library of Congress).

5. Go to **loc.gov** for more information about the PCN program.

Copyrights

Copyright coding is a mix of letters and numbers that safeguards your work. It is also optional but highly recommended. A copyright provides protection and legal recourse if someone were to plagiarize or "steal" your work.

1. You will include this copyright code on your copyright page.

2. This takes a while to obtain (7-9 months), but on the copyright page, you only need the year of the copyright.

3. Go to **copyright.gov** to register your work.

4. You can copyright your work before or after publication. Your copyright date will usually be when you completed your manuscript or published your book.

Information:
List your Copyright Number, LCCN, and ISBNs.

_____

_____

_____

_____

_____

_____

_____

_____

_____

_____

_____

_____

_____

HINT: When generating your barcode, use a 90000 code to increase or decrease your book's price to a retailer. No dollar amount will be printed above the barcode.

Step 5: Planters

This part of the process involves distributing your books. Planting your book/s in the right avenues allows your followers to grow and can assist with increasing book sales.

Distribution Services

1. Website

- Create a website. Your website is meant to sell the books that you have on hand.
- OR you can include a link to a distribution platform of your book on your website.

- OR you can create a landing page—a stand-alone web page for your book.

2. Local Retail Sales

- You will need to obtain a stockpile of books, especially if you plan to sell locally or participate in author signings, festivals, and local markets. You will sell your "author copies."

3. Amazon KDP

- Upload directly to KDP, and they will distribute your book online through Amazon.

4. Amazon Sellers Account

- Sell directly from your stockpile (Merchant Seller).
- OR, you can send books to Amazon for them to distribute (FBA- Fulfillment by Amazon). Watch out for some of the fees included in this.

5. IngramSpark

- Upload directly into your IngramSpark account, and they will distribute your book online. They work with approximately 50,000 retailers.
- This is also your connection to libraries.

6. Draft2Digital

- Upload directly into your Draft2Digital account. They distribute your book online through various retailers and other distributors.

7. Shopify

- This is beginning to be "the next best thing." I am just now starting to dive into Shopify as an option because of the variety it offers for selling products.

POD vs. Private Printer

1. A POD is a Print On Demand service.

- When a customer purchases your print book through KDP, IngramSpark, or Draft2Digital, they are printed within 1-2 days and then shipped to the customer.
- There is a percentage that each distributor takes off the top, and then you receive the remaining royalties. Your cut will depend on the cost to print your book and the customer/library/retail store that purchases your book, including your royalty agreement with the POD service.

2. A private printer will print books for you and ship them to your chosen place. Prints beforehand allow you to have a large volume ready and available for local or website sales. You are printing in bulk, so there are costs for upfront charges, but it is more beneficial for increasing profits over time. These are usually of the highest quality for printing.

3. You can order a stockpile of books from KDP, IngramSpark, and Draft2Digital at printing costs. These are called "author copies."

4. Make sure to account for shipping costs when using any of the above services. Shipping charges can be hefty.

5. Weigh and measure the cost and royalties for each print book you plan to distribute.

Links to Distributors

https://kdp.amazon.com/en_US/

https://sellercentral.amazon.com

https://www.ingramspark.com

https://draft2digital.com

https://www.shopify.com

Information:
List your chosen distribution platforms.

_____

_____

_____

_____

HINT: Order a proof book from each platform before finalizing files. You can always set a future publication date and change it when everything is ready. Any date changes must also be updated for your ISBN and LCCN metadata. Make sure the correct files are uploaded on time.

Step 6: Sun

N ow that you have chosen your distributor, it is time to create a timeline. You will need to shine a light on your book ahead of publication. You are going to work backwards.

1. When do you want to have your book out to the world? This is your release date and, in most cases, your publication date. Each platform will ask you this when uploading. Plan from 1-3 months out. Your release date can even be 6-9 months out. This time frame will give you an opportunity to prepare.

2. Create a contact sheet with family, friends, retail stores, gift shops, festivals, craft fairs, and libraries for book sales information. Make a thorough list with tentative dates, numbers, emails, and names for contact. Lists of venues should be appropriate based on your book's genre.

3. Giving books away before publication can be beneficial if they promise to give you a review on a significant platform around your publication date. Approximately 2-3 weeks before publication should be sufficient time to provide them a book.

4. Prepare a book launch. This date can be before publication, on the day, or shortly after. It can be at a house, a business, a library, a park, or anywhere else. Food, decorations, books, fun, raffles, and giveaways are all great ideas! Start planning 1-3 months ahead.

5. Ask for reviews prior to publication, and make sure the person has the link to leave a review. Include the date on which you want the review posted.

6. Use social media to spread the word. Start 1-2 months before publication.

- Create posts every few days and consistently use a "coming soon" prompt or other catchy phrase. Some posts should be "hooking the reader" (leading the horse to water).
- Create a book trailer or have someone create it for you.
- Create videos about your book that will be coming soon.

7. Have books available and be prepared to sell or give them away. Stockpiles should be received at least two weeks before launch. Carry some in your car, your briefcase, and other handy places. You always want to take advantage of an opportunity to sell a book.

8. Make a local retail sales sheet with a wholesale discount. Doing this before going to retail stores would be best. A 25-45% discount is an average wholesale price for books in bulk.

9. Use your local newspaper, radio station, and magazine company to advertise your book launch or a local signing. Usually, one media source will interview at no cost, although that is not always the case. You can use interviews as leverage to make sales to the stores if you promise to mention their business or your book signing at their venue in the interview. Trust me, it works!

**It's free advertisement for those businesses—
a win-win for you and the store!**

**Information:
Create your strategy.**

Information:
Create your timeline.
Start by month, then weeks, and then days.
Work backwards.

Information:
Start your marketing contact list.
Include Name/Business, Contact Phone, Contact Email,
Contact Date, and Notes.

HINT: Be bold when approaching a business about selling your book. I suggest you set up a meeting with the sales manager. Only do a walk-in sales pitch if the manager or staff won't contact you back.

HINT: Order print copies far in advance and scour through them with a fine-toothed comb. If there are errors, you will have time to fix them and upload them again before publication.

Step 7: Growth

Y ou are on the verge of an incredible milestone as your book is about to be released, with print copies already en route and an exciting field of dreams coming true. You have every opportunity to make your book a resounding success, just like any other author. To support your book and business growth, I have compiled a list of 12 items that will undoubtedly propel you toward success!

1. Never give up on telling others about your book. Be determined to continually make sales!

2. Utilize social media to post about your book!

3. Keep asking for reviews!

4. Create book markers and signage for your books or have a professional create them. These are great for book signings and store posters. QR codes are trendy, so adding a QR code to your signage will help gain followers and land more sales.

5. I suggest you start an LLC for your book publishing name and use this to manage your accounts. Keep in mind that there are yearly filing fees associated with this. You can visit irs.gov or make an appointment with an accountant to set up your business entity. Establish a separate bank account for book sales using your business name.

6. Create a logo or have a professional make one for you! The Logo Company and 99Designs are valid logo designers. You also can find local designers in your area and support those businesses around you.

7. Get business cards!

8. Do everything professionally! You are now a business owner *and* an author!

9. Dress appropriately when making sales for your book!

10. Consider entering your book into an award contest.

11. Go forth and make your book a success! Put in the time and effort!

12. All good things take work! You've got this! You can do this!

HINT: Above All, Enjoy Your Journey To The Top!!!

Now What? Process

Most handbooks give you the foundations to start, but do they tell you their exact process for creating the product? Well, perhaps they don't, but it's crucial. Here is an outline of the steps I took to make this book and my plans for after its publication.

The Idea

The idea for this book had been swirling in my mind for quite some time. As I worked with aspiring authors in training them on these various subjects, I knew how valuable this information was. I obtained this by watching endless videos, purchasing multiple PDF's and books, publishing our books, implementing these strategies for my clients, and researching non-stop. I was working immeasurable hours explaining and helping self-publishers create successful books, and in the meantime, creating visuals and handouts for them that would further their book's success. I thought… *Why not put these things into a book?* And then it hit me. I was once in your shoes. I didn't know what to do after my mom and I completed the manuscript of her first book. Like you, I was stuck with this question, *"Now What?"* That is where my deep dive began.

Now What? Manuscript

1. I began jotting information into my phone notes. I eventually transferred all that to a Word document via email on my computer.

2. I completed the body of the manuscript, which consisted only of basic chapter headings and paragraph flows.

3. Then, I started redesigning paragraphs, adding subheadings, and developing the theme for the book's interior—growth. It worked well because it matched our logo, vision, and mission. This also required adding this theme to the paragraphing.

4. At that point, I had the primary manuscript intact.

Manuscript Feedback

1. Feedback is essential. I wanted replies from those who have published books and others who haven't. The "bones" of the manuscript were printed or sent as a PDF and given to a few readers.

Then, I checked in with them, and their comments were invaluable. People who offer suggestions for your book or reviews before publication are known as **ARC readers** (Advanced Reader Copy) or **Beta readers**. Often, they are given copies after you have done the editing or post-formatting. Sometimes, they are given a "proof book," an ARC. I did this differently. My goal was to see if items needed clarification and other pieces needed to be included. This required input from someone earlier than a proof copy or a completely formatted version. This person can be called an **Alpha reader**.

2. I have also hired a manuscript evaluator in the past, but not for this book. An evaluator's opinion has proven to be an extremely helpful tool, so I highly suggest it for new writers. Refer to Step 2.

3. I added several things from said readers' input, reworked other sections, and then moved on to the editing.

Editing

I conducted at least two complete edits before uploading the manuscript into my formatting program. I used my "eagle eyes," Microsoft Word, Grammarly, and Prowriting Aid. Of course, there were mistakes and some rewrites based on suggestions. No one is perfect, but I strived to keep the tone of my writing within the book.

Formatting The Body

1. It took me a while to decide which program I wanted to use for formatting. Certain programs are great for young readers or novels, such as Atticus. Some are good for children's books and manuscripts that require several images (Adobe Illustrator, Photoshop, or InDesign). But for this book, I chose Vellum. Even though it is generally for novels, I knew this would have a limited number of images, primarily words and headings. Therefore, the winner was Vellum. I uploaded just the body into the program.

2. Other than editing, this is usually my most extended publishing process. I am very particular about fonts, images, uniformity, and consistency.

3. Fonts were picked from the Vellum program. I chose those that complimented the theme.

4. I added bullets, outline numbers, indentations, and alignment blocks to ensure consistency in each chapter's appearance.

5. I recreated some Canva images and used others already provided. I decided on a green and purple theme and integrated those into each illustration.

6. While formatting, I also quadruple-checked for any other errors. Viewing the manuscript in a formatted style allows you to "see things differently." Often, a paragraph or the way a sentence is structured will jump out at you. It may seem odd or out of place. If it looks or reads strangely to you, it will for the reader, too.

Title

I had yet to pick a title for my book. My business partner and I brainstormed about thirty titles until I read something to her I had written about our journey as a publishing company, and there it was: *"Now What?"* She suggested I use that as the title; the rest is history. Just kidding! It took some time to formulate the subtitle, but I think we nailed it!

Front And Back Matter Formatting

1. The front and back matter is all the extra material. I added my updated biography, copyright, introduction, other books I've written, and our PipStones Publishing information.

2. I do not scrimp on the copyright page; I make sure it's also beautifully formatted. I add all the essentials plus our logo, center every-

thing, choose a readable font, and ensure the book's necessary information is clear.

3. The blurb was prepared in a Word document so I could quickly add it when creating the cover. My partner is great at sculpting blurbs, which is no easy task. I may give her the title of Blurb Master!

4. Two ISBNs (one for print and one for ebook) were established in Bowker. I also generated one barcode for the print book. I will use my distributor's barcode for the ebook. Because I own the ebook ISBN, I can still generate a barcode from them, and they are not considered as my publisher, only the distributor. The barcode I generated for my print book will be used for all print copies, no matter if I use a POD or private print company.

5. I then registered for my LCCN through the Library of Congress's PCN program. Refer to Step 4.

6. The ISBNs and LCCN were added to the copyright page.

Finishing Touches Formatting

1. I printed a complete copy and scoured through it. I made any necessary edits and formatting changes. My partner received a copy, and she did the same.

2. I generated print (PDF) and ebook versions from my Vellum program.

3. After generating a PDF, I scanned through it, edited image sizes, moved text, and enlarged titles. This format (edition) is what will be printed, so I double-checked that everything is precisely where and how I want it to be. I also checked the ebook format.

Publication Date

1. The publication date I first picked was much further out than what I thought "could" be the date. That gave me time to prepare my

ISBNs and LCCN. I knew I needed some time to finalize files and then could act on an exact date. I entered the corrected metadata later through Bowker and my PCN account.

2. I will use the publication date to register my copyright with the Library of Congress after publication.

Cover

I outsourced my cover from a gentleman I had previously worked with. He does a great job, is reasonably priced, and has a talent for creating covers. I had too many other projects to complete this cover as my own creation and on time. Sometimes, we have to put forth money to make a great product and it's really okay to utilize other people's gifts.

Prepping On Social Media

1. I began giving hints on social media during the formatting process. Here are some examples:

- Posts about adding a new branch to our publishing company
- Posts stating, "New Book Coming Soon!"
- Posts about Editing, Formatting, Distribution, and ISBNs
- A Cover Reveal Post
- Other posts about specifics of the book
- Launch date posts

2. Preparing for a book launch: I don't try to plan my book launch too far in advance because if any errors occur in processing my files, uploading to distributors, or unexpected shipping changes, I don't want to be without books. I ensure all pieces are in place and then set my book launch. The launch date is usually decided around my publication date. I begin posting on social media while I prepare my venue and theme. This is my favorite part of the book project. Try to be

creative and integrate a theme that compliments the book's style and genre. My book launch for this book will center around plants, flowers and trees, promoting growth and vitality.

3. I usually plan author events past the publication date such as author signings, book festivals, craft fairs, and others. Refer to Step 6.

Distribution

1. I will distribute this book through Amazon, Shopify, IngramSpark, and my website, PipStones.com. The more purchasing options—the less someone can say no. If you are only going to choose one, Amazon is the most user-friendly, and of course, your landing page or website is also ideal.

2. Please note that you will make the best profit from your own books on hand, which can be obtained as author copies from a POD printer or private printer. Refer to Step 5.

3. If my book had been a children's book, I would seek out a private printer for my own copies. POD's have different requirements for children's books.

Post-Production

1. I will keep pushing the book through my social media platforms (i.e., videos, trailers, picture posts of my book, and professionally created book posts).

2. I will continue to ask for reviews and seek out book reviewers to upload reviews to Amazon and other platforms.

3. I will continue to check sales channels and develop ideas for making more sales. This includes local signings, festivals, library visits, and retail stores.

4. I will create social media ad campaigns for my book.

5. I will send information about my book to my email subscribers.

5. Remember that no matter what posts or ads you create, you must have a CTA (Call To Action). A call to action tells the viewer where you want them to go after reading your post, what link to click on, or where they can purchase your book.

Author Biography

Abigail Turner (Abby) was born in Western Nebraska, but her early childhood occurred growing up in Colorado. Her family had a plumbing and custom home-building business and traveled where the work was plentiful. Living in six different states allowed Abigail to adapt to various environments and enjoy new people.

As a former teacher for almost two decades, Abigail dedicated herself to helping others make a positive difference within their circumstances. She has always encouraged students and adults to aspire to, believe in, and develop their unique gifts and talents. Her parents and teachers instilled these values in her from a young age, and they continue to be a cornerstone in her life.

In the sixth grade, Abby began her entrepreneurial side. From lucrative lemonade stands and selling handmade bracelets to teaching private flute lessons to high schoolers, she loved the thrill of the chase and following dreams. The light had been lit!

During college, she pivoted from her flute professor's encouragement to perform full-time. Upon graduating from the University of Wyoming with a bachelor's in music education, Abby knew that helping others was primary and that she would pour herself into the art of music *and* people. She has performed with professional groups for over three decades with her primary instrument, the flute.

The collection of her experiences and attention to fine detail has contributed to her propensity to help authors, create foundations for their literary works, expand their artistic expressions, and promote their creativity.

Alabama is truly a "sweet home" for Abby. She and her husband, David, live in a small rural area in L.A. (Lower Alabama).

Abigail and her mother founded their publishing company in 2018, PipStones Publishing (PipStones, LLC).

Also by Abigail Turner

Redneck Sayin's & Terms *by Abigail Turner Paperback &*
Ebook

Redneck Sayin's & Terms is a Southern humor book inspired by her husband's
daily linguistics. Abigail moved to the South in 2006, a place she refers to as
"home." Her experiences will make you belly-laugh as you read about
hilarious moments, words, and phrases in this creative, comical book!

Redneck Sayin's & Terms on Amazon

Eskimo Joe (A Musical Journey) *by Abigail Turner:*
Hardback Children's Book

Eskimo Joe (A Musical Journey) is a fusion of fun and learning for the
family or classroom. Trek to rhythm and rhyme with Joe through a
chalk pastel panorama of Alaska. Be sure to bundle this book with its
classroom and homeschooling resource guide and downloadable
narrated music.

Eskimo Joe (Resources Guide): Spiral-Bound Classroom Book

Bundle this with the hardback book for fun, educational, and interesting additions to your classroom. Don't forget to go to our website and download the FREE narrated musical audio to accompany the books!

https://www.pipstones.com/eskimojoe

Eskimo Joe on Amazon

About PipStones Publishing

"Weavers of Tales and Tellers of Truth"

A **pip** is a seed. It's the beginning of growth and something fresh and new. Added to our name are the **stones**. These are the solid foundations that are dependable and sturdy. We believe an author must have solid foundations for their book to grow into a success.

Mission:

Our mission is to publish unique and refreshing works by various authors and genres. We aim to present and highlight literary endeavors in an ever-changing marketplace.

Vision:

Our vision is to support authors by offering essential resources and guidance in self-publishing and marketing. We believe authors should focus on their creative work without getting bogged down by the complexities of publishing logistics. We are committed to ensuring that every author has clarity and knowledge within the business of self-publishing.

Foundations:

PipStones, LLC is a mother-daughter company founded in 2018. Initially, the goal was to publish Deborah Hoffman's (the mother's) works, but they found the duo worked quite well together. They also realized there was a need to provide *author services to new and experienced writers in the publication arena. Upon extensive research and dedication, PipStones established avenues to provide services to various writers to help them reach their editing, publishing, and book marketing goals. PipStones is one of the few companies that work hand in hand with authors and help them tackle the obstacles of self-publishing.*

Services:

Editing, Formatting, Illustrations, Publishing,

Distribution, Local & Social Marketing,

Social Media Set-Up, Self-Publishing Training, and Resources

Note To An Author:

Contact us for a complimentary author consultation, and follow our social media for more book news and information!

aturner@pipstones.com

Facebook: @pipstonespublishing

TikTok: @pipstonespublishing

Instagram: @pipstones

X: @pip_stones

For videos that aid this material, or a FREE PDF to Editing Essentials, or a FREE Self-Publishing Checklist,
Go to www.pipstones.com/nwresources

To set up a complimentary consultation, scan the code or go to www.pipstones.com/contact
Let's begin your self-publishing journey!

Other Published Works:

Except A Seed *by Deborah Hoffman: Christian Mystery Novel*

The death of a young college student precipitates a quest for truth
and the eradication of an insidious evil. This is an intriguing
revelation full of twists and turns.

Except A Seed on Amazon

In Search of Justice, From Tragedy To Hope *by Ida Marie Kreiser: Memoir & Self-Help Book*

A true story of a mother who refuses to give in to the injustice surrounding the violent death of her son. This read is an open-hearted baring of the soul to help others break the bondage of devastating grief and rage.

In Search of Justice on Amazon

One Fire Animal Tales *by the Muscogee Nation of Florida:*
Children's Book

This book encompasses the rich heritage and language of the people
of one fire (The Euchee Creek). This written treasury preserves the
oral ancient tales passed down through time. As you turn the pages,
prepare to view the captivating art and the legends of The One
Above, The Master of Breath, and the things He created.

One Fire Animal Tales on Amazon

The Last Christmas Tree *by Deborah Hoffman*

The Last Christmas Tree is a treasured family gift book about a little tree named Twig, a farmer named Mr. B., and the One who is the maker of ALL things. This beautifully illustrated book imparts a lasting message for all ages and seasons.

Awards:

Gold— Christian Book Awards (Picture Book)

Gold— Royal Dragonfly Book Awards (Children's Picture Book)

Silver— Royal Dragonfly Book Awards (Best Illustrations)

Gold— Illumination Awards (Holiday Book)

Bronze— Moonbeam Book Awards (Children's Picture Book)

Honorable Mention— Readers' Favorite Awards (Picture Book)

The Last Christmas Tree also received Five-Star Editorial Reviews from Kirkus, Readers' Favorite, and Christian Book Award.

Go to: www.pipstones.com for more information.

The Last Christmas Tree on Amazon

www.ingramcontent.com/pod-product-compliance
Lightning Source LLC
Chambersburg PA
CBHW051557120626
46551CB00013B/1557